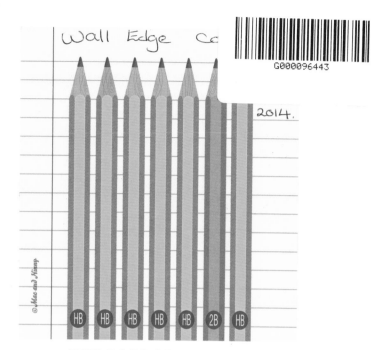

Wall Edge Co

2014.

THIS BOOK BELONGS TO

. . . .

G000096443

Bird Songs & Calls

Hannu Jännes &
Owen Roberts

NEW
HOLLAND

First published in 2011 by New Holland Publishers (UK) Ltd
London • Cape Town • Sydney • Auckland
www.newhollandpublishers.com

Garfield House, 86–88 Edgware Road, London W2 2EA, UK
80 McKenzie Street, Cape Town 8001, South Africa
Unit 1, 66 Gibbes Street, Chatswood, New South Wales, Australia 2067
218 Lake Road, Northcote, Auckland, New Zealand

10 9 8 7 6 5 4 3 2 1

ISBN 978 1 84773 779 3

Senior Editor: Krystyna Mayer
Design: Peter Gwyer
Production: Melanie Dowland
Publisher: Simon Papps

All photographs by Nigel Blake,
except (r=right; l=left): AGAMI 3, 4, 33(r), 35(l), 42(l), 43(l), 44(l), 46(r), 59(r).

Reproduction by Leo Paper Product, China
Printed and bound in China by Leo Paper Product

CONTENTS

INSIDE BACK COVER –
CD WITH 96 BIRD CALLS

INTRODUCTION TO BIRD SOUNDS

I have been watching and listening to birds for almost 50 years, but it is only in the last ten years or so, since I set up my own bird tour company, that I have had the opportunity to do so in the company of some of Europe's finest birders. It has increasingly become apparent to me not only how good they are at spotting and identifying birds from plumage features, but, even more so, how they are able to recognize all the bird sounds around them.

A few years ago I was in Africa birding with one of that continent's finest field birders. I asked him why he never carried a telescope. He held his binoculars up to me and said that he rarely needed even them, because he was usually able to identify more than 95 per cent of the birds around him simply from their songs and the calls they made. It reinforced to me just how important this aspect of birdwatching is, and I have made determined efforts in recent years to improve my knowledge of bird sounds, convinced that they are the key to better birding.

At the simplest level some species announce their name in their call, an obvious example being the familiar Cuckoo. Others birds, like many warblers, with their various similar sounding *tek*, *chek* and *kek* calls, take many years to achieve familiarity with. The aim of this book and CD is to give relatively novice birdwatchers the chance to relate the appearance of almost a hundred of Britain's most common birds to their songs and calls, and by doing so to enhance the enjoyment to be had from observing the daily spectacle of birds in our surroundings.

Owen Roberts

Dippers employ a rapid whirring flight, often low over water.

HOW TO USE THIS BOOK

- This book, together with the CD, teaches you to recognize some of the amazing sounds our birds make. The book features a photograph and some information on each of the 96 birds. It tells you where to find them, if they are here all year or only visiting us, what they eat and how they nest.

- Use the CD with the book to match the pictures of the birds with the sounds they make. The track numbers on the CD correspond with the numbering of the birds in the book.
- As you learn and remember the sounds, you will be able to look for those birds when you hear them. Simply follow the call and look for the bird that is making it.

CD track number and common name of bird.

Icons indicating food and nesting information.

Information about the call and the corresponding track number.

10 | Pochard

The Pochard is a medium-sized diving duck that is scarce as a breeder in Britain but common in winter, when the population increases with migrants from northern and eastern Europe. The handsome drake has a grey back, a black chest and stern, and a bright chestnut head with a black bill that has a grey band. Females have a similar pattern, but of dull greys and browns. Pochards are usually seen on larger lakes and reservoirs. They feed mainly by dabbling and diving.

 Aquatic plants, molluscs, water insects and small fish.

 Builds a bulky nest of rank vegetation, often so close to water that it has to be raised up like that of a Coot.

 TRACK N° 10
Rarely heard. First display calls of male including nasal *aaaooochaaa* and more commonly heard 3–4 short sharp whistles, *ki–ki–ki–ki*. Then loud purring call of female.

11 | Tufted Duck

The jaunty little Tufted Duck is the most common diving duck in Britain. The dapper black and white drake has a head tuft that is longer in spring than at other times. The female is similarly patterned, but brown replaces the black and grey-brown the white. The bill is blue with a black tip in adults of both sexes. Tufted Ducks are common inland on lakes and large ponds, especially in winter when they also frequent salt-water habitats.

 Aquatic plants and invertebrates, including crustaceans, small molluscs and insect larvae.

 Builds a nest of dry grass and sedges with a down lining, usually well hidden in dry situations near water.

TRACK N° 11
First display call of male, a quick, bubbly series of accelerating notes on a slightly falling pitch. Then growling calls typical of *Aythya* genus females.

12

1 | Great Crested Grebe

Grebes live their lives on or very close to water. A Great Crested Grebe's sleek body shape is ideal for diving to catch aquatic prey. Its body approaches that of a Mallard in size, with a long and slender neck. Brown above and white below, with a long pale pink bill, in summer it develops brownish-red, black-tipped head plumes. These are used to good effect during its elaborate spring courtship displays. In summer Great Crested Grebes breed on inland waters, but at other times they are found mainly on the open sea.

 Small fish, frogs, molluscs and aquatic insects, which it catches by diving.

 Builds a large floating structure of wet decayed weeds and reeds, loosely moored to aquatic vegetation.

TRACK N° 01

Various loud calls from a breeding colony.

2 | Little Grebe

This is Britain's smallest grebe. It has a rounded body, whitish vent and short bill with a pale vent. In winter it is drab brown above and buffish-white below, in summer blackish-brown with chestnut cheeks and foreneck; in all plumages there is a fluffy pale stern. Little Grebes are well known for their loud whinneying call. Pairs display in duet. In summer they are found in all types of freshwater habitat, but in winter they favour larger areas of open water such as lakes and reservoirs.

 Small fish, molluscs and aquatic insects. Dives to catch its prey.

 Nest comprises a floating collection of underwater weeds loosely anchored to aquatic vegetation.

TRACK N° 02

Mix of far-carrying, rattling, high-pitched trills and a high-pitched single note. Calls *bit*.

| Grey Heron

Heron in tree (left); in flight (right).

The only common heron species in Britain and the largest European heron, the Grey Heron is a resident that can occur almost anywhere near water. It is a large yellow-billed, grey, white and black bird nearly a metre tall, which is often seen standing by shallow water or in a wet field. Adults have two broad black stripes at the back of the crown, which extend into slim black head plumes in the breeding season, when the bill also acquires a pinkish hue. Juveniles are slightly stockier and plainer with less contrast than adults.

In flight the Grey Heron looks huge, with its neck drawn in, hunched between its shoulders, and its long legs trailing beyond its tail. Its wingbeats are slow and ponderous.

Grey Herons are found year round in marshes, ponds, lakes, rivers, canals, flooded fields and estuaries throughout Europe. They are usually solitary, although several birds may feed close together, generally close to the shore or a bank.

Adults display around nest platforms, employing bill snapping and a variety of blood-curdling calls. Young in nests maintain continuous loud clicking calls.

 Fish, frogs, newts and beetles, but also takes small mammals and the young of ground-nesting birds. Hunts by stalking slowly through shallow water, or standing motionless waiting for prey to come within reach, when it strikes with lightning speed.

 Nests colonially in branches of tall trees, building a huge shallow platform of sticks. A nest is added to each year until it finally topples. Massive old nests may be a metre across and may also provide homes for nesting Tree Sparrows.

TRACK N° 03

Various harsh raucous flight calls based around a croaking *kark.*

4 | Mute Swan

Courting swans (left); swan bathing (right)

Familiar to many people from childhood visits to a park, the Mute Swan is a huge white bird with an orange bill that has a black knob at the base. At 152cm in length, it is the largest flying bird in Britain. Juveniles are grey-brown, becoming progressively more white as they mature, a process that takes about two years to complete.

The Mute Swan often arches its wings as it swims, looking like a stately white galleon as it glides effortlessly on the calm waters of the large open ponds, lakes, rivers and even still coastal waters it inhabits. In flight its wings make a loud throbbing sound. It is found across northern and western Europe, and is resident in Britain.

Swans frequently mate for life and breed in the same place year after year. Established pairs engage in elaborate courtship displays in spring.

Although the Mute Swan can be very tame and takes bread from humans, an approach to its nest will soon arouse aggression involving mock attacks and raised wings, accompanied by loud grunts and hisses. Male swans (cobs) are particularly aggressive in the breeding season, and guard the eggs whenever the female (pen) leaves the nest. Very young swans (cygnets) may be carried around on the backs of their mothers.

 Water plants and also grazes grass, especially in winter. Usually feeds on water by dipping its neck below the surface, sometimes upending. May also feed in groups in meadows and fields.

 Constructs a huge mound of rank vegetation or seaweed close to water.

TRACK N° 04

First a snorting *heeorr*, then a loud throbbing sound with each wingbeat in flight.

| Mallard

6 | Wigeon

y far the most common and most frequently
een duck in Britain, the Mallard is resident
herever there is fresh water. The birds often
terbreed with farmyard ducks so they can
e quite variable, but pure-bred birds are easy
identify. The male has a glossy green head
nd neck, a rusty-brown breast and a bright
ellow bill. The female is a rather more drab
ariegated brown all over. A dabbling duck,
ie Mallard feeds by upending to immerse
s head below the water's surface. Mallards
re found anywhere near fresh water around
onds, ditches and streams.

The Wigeon is a medium-sized duck that
is mainly a winter visitor to Britain from
more northerly climes. The male has grey
upperparts, a white belly, a pinkish chest,
and a bright chestnut neck and head topped
with a creamy-yellow forehead and crown.
The female is a plainer assortment of browns,
but shares the male's white belly and blue-
grey bill. In winter Wigeons are found mainly
on coasts and estuarine marshes, where they
graze the short grasses, and also on some
lakes and reservoirs. They have a far-carrying
whistling call.

 Omnivorous. Mallards eat plant matter,
worms, snails, insects and shellfish.
Birds used to humans will take bread.

 Water plants and grasses.

 Constructs a nest of grass and dead
leaves lined with duck down in a wide
range of sites, but always in good
ground cover near water.

 Builds a nest lined with down close
to water and well hidden in grass
and other dense vegetation.

TRACK N° 05
Series of loud quacks by female. The
much quieter calls of a feeding flock include
lower pitched and softer calls by male, and a sharp
wiu-whistle by male when guarding female.

TRACK N° 06
Loud whistling *wee-oo* by male. Then
whistles by male and harsh calls by females
when courting. Finally a short *raah* call,
commonly heard outside the courting period.

7 | Gadwall

Slightly smaller than the Mallard, the female Gadwall is very much like the duck of that species save for a dark-centred bill with yellow sides. The drake can also appear rather plain, but closer inspection reveals a grey body that has fine pencil lines (vermiculations) of black. The stern is black, the head pale brown and the speculum white. Gadwalls are local but increasing as breeders in Britain. Their numbers are supplemented with immigrants from the north and east in winter. They are found in a variety of fresh and brackish water locations.

 Mainly aquatic plants.

 Constructs a nest of grass and dry plants lined with down, well concealed near water.

8 | Shoveler

This is a Mallard-sized duck characterized by a massive spatulate bill. The male has a glossy dark green head, a white breast, chestnut flanks, and a black back and stern. The female is a mix of mottled browns. Shovelers are not uncommon on shallow lakes, marshland meadows and flooded grasslands. Numbers in Britain are swelled in winter by immigrants from north-east Europe and Iceland.

 Seeds and aquatic plants, small crustaceans, molluscs and insects. Feeds in shallow water, sieving food through its bill.

 Nest is well concealed in often dry vegetation, but with water close by.

 TRACK N° **07**

First a quacking call like the Mallard's by female, then a high-pitched whistle, *pee*, in courtship and finally low croaking *ahrk* calls by male.

 TRACK N° **08**

Nasal, disyllabic call of male, which is the most commonly heard call. Then female's version of the same call.

Teal

Male (left); pair with female in foreground (right).

 e Teal is Britain's smallest dabbling duck. At distance the male's head looks all-dark, but ose up it can be seen to be chestnut with rk green sides narrowly bordered yellow. s body is basically grey with a dark-speckled eamy breast, and with conspicuous dark llow stern patches. A white flash on its de is conspicuous, even from far away. e female is a dowdy mix of mottled browns. on-breeding males, in eclipse plumage, ok like the females, but are more uniform colour, with a darker head and vestigial ce markings. Both sexes have grey bills. veniles look much like females, but have stronger pattern.

Teals frequently call with a high ringing ek. They are quick to flush and rise almost rtically from the water, and fast in flight, ying very low. They are common birds, pecially in winter, on still or slow-moving esh water with fringing vegetation such s lakes, reservoirs and estuaries. Highly regarious outside the breeding season, they form large flocks that may feed in the open in mud or nearby grazing meadows. They feed by dabbling, upending or grazing, and occasionaly even dive to reach food.

 Mainly aquatic invertebrates, such as crustaceans, insects and worms, in the breeding season, and seeds and plants in winter.

 Nest is lined with down, and concealed in thick cover in both wet and dry situations. May nest some distance from water. The tiny young weigh just 15 grams at hatching.

TRACK N°   09

First calls of single male, then of an excited group of males courting female. Finally calls of female.

10 | Pochard

The Pochard is a medium-sized diving duck that is scarce as a breeder in Britain but common in winter, when the population increases with migrants from northern and eastern Europe. The handsome drake has a grey back, a black chest and stern, and a bright chestnut head with a black bill that has a grey band. Females have a similar pattern, but of dull greys and browns. Pochards are usually seen on larger lakes and reservoirs. They feed mainly by dabbling and diving.

 Aquatic plants, molluscs, water insects and small fish.

 Builds a bulky nest of rank vegetation, often so close to water that it has to be raised up like that of a Coot.

11 | Tufted Duck

The jaunty little Tufted Duck is the most common diving duck in Britain. The dapper black and white drake has a head tuft that is longer in spring than at other times. The female is similarly patterned, but brown replaces the black and grey-brown the white. The bill is blue with a black tip in adults of both sexes. Tufted Ducks are common inland on lakes and large ponds, especially in winter when they also frequent salt-water habitats.

 Aquatic plants and invertebrates, including crustaceans, small molluscs and insect larvae.

 Builds a nest of dry grass and sedges with a down lining, usually well hidden in dry situations near water.

TRACK N° 10

Rarely heard. First display calls of male including nasal *aaaooochaaa* and more commonly heard 3–4 short sharp whistles, *ki-ki-ki-ki*. Then loud purring call of female.

TRACK N° 11

First display call of male, a quick, bubbly series of accelerating notes on a slightly falling pitch. Then growling calls typical of *Aythya* genus females.

2 | Sparrowhawk

Male (left); female (right).

he Sparrowhawk is now resident in most wooded parts of Britain, and is the second most common raptor after the Kestrel. It is a rather small bird of prey with a long tail and short broad wings. Male and female birds differ markedly in plumage and size.

The male has blue-grey upperparts, russet cheeks, finely barred orange-red underparts, dark bars on the tail and dark wing-tips. The upper parts of the female are mainly dark brown, and she has white underparts with fine grey-brown horizontal bars, pale 'eyebrows' and a whitish tail with darker bars. She is 25 per cent larger than the male. Juveniles are brownish, and reach sexual maturity at between one and three years of age.

Sparrowhawks are birds of open countryside with woods and, increasingly, of suburban gardens. They are found across Europe, and are mainly resident in Britain. They typically fly in a shallow flap and glide,

and do not hover like many other birds of prey. The Sparrowhawk population declined dramatically in the second half of the 20th century, coinciding with the introduction of certain insecticides. Following their banning in 1975, numbers have increased.

 Long tail and short wings provide excellent manoeuvrability, allowing the bird to move at speed through wooded areas to snatch small birds like tits, finches and sparrows by surprise. Females also take larger birds such as Woodpigeons.

 A substantial platform of twigs is erected in a broadleaved or coniferous tree, often based on the remains of an old crow's nest or squirrel's drey.

TRACK N° 12

Only vocal near nest during breeding season, producing a quiet chattering *keh-keh-keh-keh*. Recently fledged juveniles utter loud and demanding *kee-kee-kee-kee* begging calls.

13

13 | Common Buzzard

A large raptor with very broad wings, the Common Buzzard is basically dark brown with variable amounts of white on the underbody and wings. It has a heavy slow flight, and when soaring holds its wings in a shallow V. Common Buzzards have increased in recent decades due to a reduction in persecution, and are now found in many wooded areas that have access to open country where they can hunt.

 Small mammals, especially young rabbits, and carrion, frogs, worms and beetles.

 Constructs a bulky stick nest in a tree, or occasionally on a ledge on a crag or coastal cliff.

14 | Hobby

This handsome medium-sized falcon is a summer visitor from Africa. The female is larger than the male, but otherwise the sexe are alike, with slate-grey upperparts, pale, heavily streaked underparts, rusty thighs and under-tail, and white chin and cheeks with black moustaches. Long pointed wings and a short tail give the bird the appearance of a huge swift in flight. A heath and open woodland raptor, it has increased in recent years, spreading north and west from south-east England strongholds.

 Catches small birds, including swallow and martins, and large insects in flight

 Generally uses an old crow's nest in a spinney or open woodland.

TRACK N° 13

Quite vocal for a bird of prey, particularly in the breeding season. Mewing plaintive calls are usually uttered in flight, but also while perched.

TRACK N° 14

Two versions of the rather high and strangled *kew-kew-kew...* or *keer-keer-keer*, usually only heard near nest.

5 | Kestrel

The Kestrel is Britain's most common bird of prey, often seen hanging in the air on quivering wings, especially over motorway verges. Both sexes have rich warm brown backs and grey rumps and tails, and the male has a grey head. Juveniles are similar to females, but are usually more yellowish-brown. Kestrels are often seen crouching on roadside wires and lamp posts, presenting a long-tailed outline. They are resident throughout Britain.

 Rodents, especially voles. It will also take insects, but lacks sufficient speed to catch birds.

 Nests on ledges of cliffs or buildings, and in tree holes and old crows' nests.

16 | Pheasant

Native to eastern Asia, the Pheasant was introduced to Britain about a thousand years ago. The male is unmistakable, with his green head, the bare red skin on his face and his very long tail. The female is a more subdued brown with dark spots. Pheasants are resident in open woodland, farmland with dense cover and large gardens in rural areas. They are most common in areas where they are artificially reared for the shoot. When disturbed they typically rise with a clatter and whirring of wings.

 Seeds, fruits, berries, roots and insects.

 Nests in a depression sparsely lined with grass and leaves in good ground cover.

TRACK N° 15

Rapid series of sharp *kee-kee-kee-kee* notes, first uttered by male, followed by slightly coarser calls by female.

TRACK N° 16

Display call of male is a loud, far-carrying *karck-kah*, normally followed by a quick audible whirr of wings. Another call (not on CD) is a loud *kh'kh'kh...*, uttered by both sexes.

17 | Grey Partridge

This game bird was formerly a common sight on Britain's farmlands, but modern farming methods have led to a significant decline in its population. The sexes are a similar grey-brown above and grey below, with chestnut-barred flanks, an orange face and throat, and a blackish horseshoe-shaped belly patch. Grey Partridges fly close to the ground, producing a whirring sound with their wings. Outside the breeding season they form small flocks known as coveys.

 Seeds and leaves with some insects when available.

 Nest is well concealed in thick vegetation below a hedgerow. Lays large clutches of up to 20 eggs.

18 | Water Rail

The Water Rail is not uncommon, especially in winter, when numbers are increased by migrants from the north and east, but it is rarely seen due to its secretive nature and preferred dense reed and sedge habitat. However, its repertoire of loud grunts and squeals is often heard. It looks like a small Moorhen with long legs and a bill that is conspicuously red. Often only the pale buff under-tail is seen as the bird retreats hurriedly into cover.

 Insects, worms and crustaceans. Also feeds on plant matter, such as shoots, roots and seeds, particularly during autumn and winter.

 Nest is often constructed over water in densely vegetated situations. It is raised above the water by a platform of bent and broken reed stems.

TRACK N° **17**
Two different versions of the most commonly heard harsh call, traditionally likened to the sound of a rusty gate. Then a short series of calls by an individual taking off.

TRACK N° **18**
First the courtship call used by both sexes, a long rhythmic series of sharp notes, *ghik-ghik-ghik-ghik*, then the far-carrying 'pig squeal' used for display, alarm and territorial purposes.

9 | Moorhen

The Moorhen is sometimes confused with the larger Coot. It is a blackish and slate-grey water bird with a bright red, yellow-tipped bill and a conspicuously white under-tail. It is mainly resident, and common where there are ponds, small lakes, waterside meadows, canals, and slow-moving rivers and streams that have nearby dense vegetation. Moorhens swim with a series of jerky head and tail movements, and when feeding on land eck in a hen-like way.

 Aquatic plants, molluscs, insects, worms, seeds and grass.

 Nest is built of reeds, grass and sedges just out of water.

20 | Coot

The Coot is a familiar black water bird with a conspicuous white bill with a white 'shield' above it, found in most open freshwater habitats that have surrounding vegetation in which to nest and shelter. When swimming it employs a noticeable forwards nod of the head with each paddle. On land its pale legs and huge lobed feet are conspicuous. It forms flocks, which are sometimes large, outside the breeding season.

 Dives for water plants, and insect and small animal matter.

 Constructs a large structure of reeds and sedges in waterside vegetation, sometimes actually in the water, but raised above it.

TRACK N° 19

The various calls include a nasal *prrruwkk* and sharp, rubber toy-like *kwe-ick*.

TRACK N° 20

Short, high-pitched, explosive *ihh* or *piip*, then a short sharp *kuh* or *geowh*. At the end a quite loud and often repeated, more conversationally given *egh-ekh-ekh-ekh*.

21 | Little Ringed Plover

This wading bird is a summer visitor from Africa. It first bred in Britain, where it is confined to sand and gravel areas by fresh water, as recently as 1938, doubtless aided by the proliferation of gravel pits in modern times. It is very similar to the more common Ringed Plover, but smaller with dull pinkish-grey legs, a yellow orbital eye-ring and an all-dark bill. In flight it is easily distinguished from the Ringed Plover because it lacks this species' wing-bar.

 Mainly invertebrates in summer, and marine worms, crustaceans and molluscs in winter.

 Nest is a simple scrape in sand or gravel. Characteristically of plovers, parent birds may feign a broken wing if they sense a threat to their nest or chicks, in order to divert predators.

TRACK N° 21

First the song, then calls, and at the end harsher and shorter warning calls.

22 | Golden Plover

In winter the Golden Plover is found in large flocks on wet fields and estuaries, but in summer, when it sports golden-spangled upperparts and a black face, breast and belly it breeds on moors, upland pastures and mountains. It has a plaintive whistling call evocative of wild places. In Britain numbers increase considerably in winter with migrant from colder regions.

 Mainly insects and worms, with some seeds and berries. Feeds extensively at night.

 Nest is a simple scrape in heather or rough grass.

TRACK N° 22

First *per-wheo per-wheo...* song in song flight, then another display call, a cyclical *whe-wheedli'whe-wheedli...*, then calls on breeding grounds.

3 | Lapwing

arge flocks of Lapwings are a common sight n winter on open fields and marshes, but ne birds' spectacular springtime aerobatic isplays over rough pastures are now much ss commonly seen than they once were due o changes in farming methods. The bird is istinctive, with white underparts, a black hest, unique iridescent green upperparts, ink legs and a head topped by a long and whispy erectile crest. The common country ame Peewit is an interpretation of its call.

 Mainly adult and larval insects, spiders, snails and worms.

 Nest is a simple sparsely lined scrape in pasture or arable land.

24 | Dunlin

The Dunlin is common in winter and on migration along shores and estuaries. In summer most birds leave Britain, but a few remain to breed on high moors. Starling-sized, the Dunlin is grey above and white below, with the breast streaked darker, but in summer the upperparts become rufous-brown and a prominent black patch develops on the belly. At all times the rather long and gently decurved bill is a good identification feature.

 Small molluscs, crustaceans and worms in winter, but mainly insects in summer.

 Builds a cup of grass well hidden in moorland grass or heather.

TRACK N° 23

First various sounds, including wingbeats and calls, by male in display flight, then warning calls by adult bird.

TRACK N° 24

First a series of scolding, growling *churr'eeeer–eeeer–eeeer...*, followed by a long, descending growling trill. Both are songs.

25 | Curlew

This is the large grey-brown wader with an extremely long and down-curved bill that is a familiar sight in coastal areas in winter. In summer it breeds on moors, upland pastures and, more rarely nowadays, lowland wet meadows. It is known throughout the year for its loud and melancholy fluty whistle, and in summer for a bubbling trill during its nuptial song flights.

 Molluscs and mud worms in winter, and insects and moorland berries in summer.

 Nests in a slight depression in grass tussocks or heather.

26 | Redshank

A medium-sized wader, grey-brown above and white below outside the breeding season, the Redshank becomes darker above and more streaked below when breeding. Its longish red legs (shanks) and red bill-base are always good identification marks. A nervous species, it is often the first bird to rise shrieking in alarm when disturbed. It is mainly coastal in winter and on migration, when breeding birds frequent wet meadows, grass moors and coastal marshes.

 Mainly molluscs and crustaceans, but insects when breeding.

 Nest is constructed of grasses woven into a dome, and sited in a dry situation.

TRACK N° **25**

Series of 'curlew' calls, and at the end the rising bubbling song.

TRACK N° **26**

First a monosyllabic *tjuu* and disyllabic *tjuu-u* calls, then the song.

27 | Common Sandpiper

Brown above and white below with densely streaked sides to its breast, when seen the Common Sandpiper crouches forwards and constantly bobs its rather elongated rear. Its flight involves rapid wingbeats interspersed with short glides, showing white wing-bars and calling constantly. A summer visitor from Africa, it breeds along upland streams, river banks and lake shores, but on passage it can be seen in all wet habitats including coasts and estuaries.

 Small molluscs, crustaceans, insects and worms.

 Nest is a scrape in sand or gravel close to water.

28 | Woodcock

The Woodcock is a large (body size almost that of a Woodpigeon) and attractively patterned, reddish-brown wader with a long thick bill. Unlike most waders, it favours woodland with damp areas where it can probe for food. It is difficult to see, being active only at dawn and dusk, the exception being in spring when it patrols its territory at dusk in a low flight called 'roding', bill pointed downwards, over the treetops. When flushed in woodland it rises with a sound likened to tearing cloth.

 Worms, insects and larvae.

 Nest is a depression in leaf litter or brambles, usually in damp and shaded woodland.

 TRACK N° **27**

First the song, then a single flight call, followed by a series of alarm calls.

 TRACK N° **28**

Two series of the distinctive 'roding' song flight.

21

29 | Snipe

A medium-sized wader, the Snipe is richly patterned in browns and buffs, with dark-barred flanks and a white belly. Its head is striped black and buff, and its bill is very long in relation to its size. When flushed it rises with an explosive call, and zigzags away before towering high above the interloper. Snipes frequent all manner of damp habitats, especially in winter, when there is considerable immigration of birds from colder countries.

 Mainly worms and insects.

 Constructs a grass-lined cup, usually in tussocks amid boggy ground.

30 | Black-headed Gull

This is a common and widespread small gull that is grey above and white below. Its name is a misnomer, because the head is actually chocolate-brown, and then only in the breeding season, with the dark colour decreasing to a mere ear-spot in winter. It is not confined to the seashore and may be abundant inland near water, where it will readily come to take bread.

 Often follows the plough, feeding on disturbed worms and insects, but also takes grain, scraps and invertebrates.

 Nests colonially, sometimes in large numbers, in tussocks or on flat ground by lakes, ponds and coastal marshes.

TRACK N° **29**
First the drumming sound by male (twice), then two series of the loud rhythmic *chic-chip-chip-chip...*, and at the end a series of characteristic *scaap* flight calls.

TRACK N° **30**
Very vocal, particularly at breeding colonies and feeding sites. Slurred screeching calls, initially by a single individual, then the cacophony of a breeding colony.

1 | Common Tern

Terns are seabirds with a slender build, long
pointed wings and long and deeply forked
tails. The Common Tern has grey wings and
back, with white underparts that become
greyer in the breeding season, a black cap,
red legs and a red bill with a black tip.
A summer visitor to Britain from Africa
frequenting low-lying shores and inland lakes
and rivers, it will readily nest on artificial
floating raft platforms.

 Small fish.

 Nests colonially on sand, pebbles
and gravel, where it makes a small
scrape in which to lay its eggs.

32 | Stock Dove

The Stock Dove is resident in open woodland,
parkland, town parks and gardens with
mature trees throughout Britain apart from
the west and north of Scotland. It lacks
the white on the wing and neck of the
Woodpigeon, and employs a flitting rather
than a powerful wing action in flight. It is
similar to some feral pigeons, but is rarely
found in their preferred habitats.

 Grains, weeds (especially charlock),
young shoots and seedlings.

 Nests in holes in trees, ruined farm
buildings and even old rabbit burrows.

 TRACK N° 31

First various harsh calls by breeding birds,
then calls of adult and juvenile.

 TRACK N° 32

A deep two-note advertising call,
ooo-wuhh-ooo-wuh, which is repeated
8–9 times in a series.

33 | Feral Pigeon

This feral descendant of the now rare Rock Dove is the common pigeon of Britain's town and city streets, parks and gardens. Some birds remain true to their ancestral form and are pale grey with black wing-bars and a white rump, but interbreeding with lost homing pigeons has resulted in a wide variety of plumage colours, including some with a considerable amount of white, brown or even black.

 Grain, seeds and bread from humans.

 Wild Rock Doves nest on rocky coasts and mountain cliffs. Feral pigeons replicate this habitat, using ledges on buildings and in ruins for their nests.

34 | Woodpigeon

The Woodpigeon is found throughout Britain wherever there are trees or large bushes in which to roost and nest in. A bulky grey pigeon with white patches on its neck and wings, it takes off with a loud clatter of wings. Woodpigeons are often seen in display flights, during which they climb rapidly to a height, clap their wings, then glide slowly downwards. They are resident in Britain, and the population is augmented in winter with many more individuals from continental Europe.

 Seeds, clover, peas and cereals throughout the year, with beechmast and acorns in autumn.

 Builds a flimsy platform of twigs, which is easily seen from below, in a tree, bush or large hedge.

TRACK N° 33

Various very deep and hollow-sounding cooing sounds that are not very far carrying in the noisy environment in which they live.

TRACK N° 34

The commonly heard song or advertising call is a deep five-syllable hooting, with a very characteristic rhythm.

35 | Collared Dove

nknown in Britain until 50 years ago, the
ollared Dove spread rapidly across Europe
om Asia in the 1900s, and is now common
nd widespread. It particularly favours parks
nd gardens in towns, and farms and villages
n rural areas. A small slim dove with pale
uff plumage relieved only by black wing-
ps and a black collar, it often perches on
oadside wires, roofs and chimneys.

 Seeds and grain. The species' rapid
expansion across Europe has been
attributed to its exploitation of
sources of spilt grain.

 Erects a platform nest in a dense tree,
usually a conifer, near farms, in town
parks and gardens, and in villages..

36 | Cuckoo

Best known for its call, the Cuckoo is a fairly
large bird, grey above and whitish below,
and heavily barred darker. In flight the
long tail and pointed wings are obvious
identification marks. A summer visitor to
Britain from tropical Africa, the Cuckoo
can be found in a wide variety of open
habitats with bushes and trees where it has
the opportunity to parasitise the nests of
host species, especially those of Meadow
Pipits, Reed Warblers and Dunnocks.

 Insects and especially hairy caterpillars.

 Lays one egg in the nest of the host
species. The resultant hatchling ejects
the eggs/young of the hosts and is
raised by them.

TRACK N° 35

The commonly heard advertising call
is a repeated trisyllabic hollow cooing with
a characteristic rhythm. A thin nasal *eerrrr*
(not on CD) is given in flight and in excitement.

 TRACK N° 36

First the song, then the bubbling
call made by female.

37 | Tawny Owl

The owl that hoots, this bird is more often heard than seen. Medium-sized and brown mottled with black and buff, it occurs where there are large mature trees, including in large suburban gardens. Strictly nocturnal, it is most often seen in the headlights of vehicles. More rarely it is chanced upon at a daytime roost in a tree hole or pressed close against a tree trunk, its presence often betrayed by the small birds that are mobbing it.

 Largely small mammals, especially mice, but also small birds and insects, and occasionally young rabbits and squirrels.

 Usually nests in a hollow tree, but also in rocks, old crows' nests and even rabbit holes.

38 | Common Swift

The only swift species commonly occurring in Britain, the Common Swift is a summer visitor from southern Africa, spending only a very short time in Britain from late April/early May to early September. It is unmistakable, with a short forked tail and long scythe-shaped wings, and appears all-black at a distance. It is perfectly adapted to life in the air and rarely lands other than at the nest, even sleeping on the wing. Swifts can be seen on summer evenings as they 'scream' through towns and villages.

 Insects caught on the wing.

 Nests colonially beneath roof tiles, and in holes in eaves and church towers.

TRACK N° **37**
Song is a series of hollow-sounding hooting notes: a strong hoot, a pause, a short hoot, then a shivering sequence of rapid *hoo*-ing. Contact call is a loud sharp *ke-vick*.

TRACK N° **38**
First the shrill, screaming flight calls, then (similar) calls from birds roosting at their nest holes.

9 | Green Woodpecker

striking woodpecker nearly as big as a ckdaw, this bird is green with a red crown nd a yellow rump. It has an unmistakable ounding flight, closing its wings after ery few beats, and to top it all has a nique manic call. It climbs trees in jerky ops, but unlike most European woodpeckers so feeds readily on the ground. Green oodpeckers are resident and widely but inly distributed in Britain in areas with attered mature trees.

 Wood-boring larvae in trees, while on the ground the long and sticky tongue is adept at sweeping up ants. In winter it also feeds on berries, nuts and acorns.

 Excavates a relatively large hole in a tree.

40 | Great Spotted Woodpecker

A predominantly black and white woodpecker, the male has a red crown, and both sexes have red under-tails. It is as large as a Starling (Britain's only other pied woodpecker, the Lesser Spotted, is sparrow-sized), and common in woodland, parks and gardens even on the urban fringe. Its loud rapid drumming is a regularly heard country sound, made by banging the bill against dead trees, telegraph poles and even metal objects. It rarely visits the ground, but is frequent at bird tables.

 Wood-boring larvae, insects and, in winter, conifer seeds.

 Excavates a hole in a tree that is much smaller than that of the Green Woodpecker.

TRACK N° 39

First two sets of yaffling *hwahwahwahwa* calls, followed by two sets of chuckling flight calls.

TRACK N° 40

First drumming (made by both sexes), which is short and fades towards the end. Then the *kick* call heard throughout the year.

41 | Skylark

The Skylark is known for its song, but to look at it is a rather nondescript greyish-brown bird with darker streaks and a whitish belly. The often raised crown crest is a conspicuous feature. Resident in Britain, the population is augmented in winter by birds from the north and east. Skylarks can be common on farmland, heaths, meadows, moors, coastal marshes and dunes, and form flocks in winter on stubble and ploughed land. Declines in their populations in Britain are thought to be due to agricultural intensification.

 Insects, weeds and seeds.

 Constructs a simple cup of dried grass in grassland or crops, often in the hoofprint of a cow or horse.

42 | Swallow

This bird is a common sight in the countryside around farms and villages. It has blue-black upper feathers and pale buff under feathers, which are relieved only by a bright chestnut chin, as well as long tail streamers. Summer visitors to Britain from southern Africa, Swallows frequently line telegraph wires in autumn before flying south.

 Almost exclusively insects taken on the wing.

 Swallows originally built a cup of mud in a cave or on rocks, but have evolved a close association with humans and now erect their nests in outbuildings, porches and sheds instead.

 TRACK N° **41**

First the song, which consists of a lengthy outpouring of chirrups and whistles given at height, then *pruit* flight calls.

TRACK N° **42**

Melodious twittering and sputtering song, interspersed with a strangled croak, followed by a trilling rattle. Females use the length of the rattle to evaluate the fitness of the males.

43 | House Martin

A summer visitor to Britain from tropical Africa, the House Martin is similar to the Swallow in being blue-black above and white below, but it has a more compact shape and lacks tail streamers, and has a very conspicuous white rump. It frequents towns, villages and farms with a nearby supply of soft mud for the construction of its nest with something to build it on.

 Insects taken on the wing, but usually at a much higher level than those taken by the Swallow.

 Nests colonially, building a cup of mud attached to a building, bridge or cliff.

44 | Sand Martin

A summer visitor from Africa, this is the only brown-backed martin found in Britain. It is white below and has a distinctive brownish breast band separating the white throat and breast. A colonial breeder in sand and gravel pits, and also where other suitable banks exist (rivers and cliffs), it feeds aerially by catching tiny insects, usually over water. On migration it roosts communally in reed beds.

 Small insects, which are taken on the wing.

 Excavates a tunnel in a sand or earth bank. The tunnel is excavated at a rate of 8–10cm a day, and may be up to a metre in length.

TRACK N° **43**

Short, dry stony rattles by birds visiting their nests.

TRACK N° **44**

First calls from a small breeding colony, then calls of a big flock of birds catching insects low over water.

45 | Tree Pipit

The Tree Pipit is very like the Meadow Pipit, but it has a plainer back and the streaking on its breast is finer and less obvious. It frequents more wooded areas, but this characteristic cannot be relied upon to distinguish it from its close relative. Its call and song are very different. A summer visitor from Africa, it breeds in various types of woodland, in Britain especially in young conifer plantations. It employs a characteristic parachuting song flight, usually from and to a tree, with the song becoming more drawn out at the end.

 Insects and occasionally seeds.

 Builds a nest of grass well concealed in a tussock on the ground.

46 | Meadow Pipit

This is a small olive-brown bird, which is streaked darker above and whitish-buff below with black streaks. Its legs are noticeably pinkish. It is common throughout Britain in open country, especially on heaths and moors, and in coastal grasslands. During its spring display it flies up from the ground to a height, before parachuting back down to the ground, singing throughout. In contrast to the song of the Tree Pipit, the Meadow Pipit's song speeds up at the end of its song flight.

 Insects, small worms and some seeds.

 Constructs a neat and closely woven cup of grass well hidden in heather, rough grass, rushes or tussocks.

TRACK N° **45**
Song, first three strophes uttered by a bird sitting in a tree top, then a fourth, longer and more complicated strophe given in song flight. At the end two buzzing flight calls.

TRACK N° **46**
Song of a parachuting bird repeats the *tsiltsilptsilptsliptsilp* theme, and *ist istt* calls are usually given on taking flight.

7 | Yellow Wagtail

im and long-tailed like all wagtails,
is summer visitor from Africa has a
rey-brown back and yellow underparts,
hich are bright in the male and less so
the female. The colour of the head is
ictated by geography. In Britain the Yellow
agtail's head is greenish-brown with a
ellow supercillium and throat. The head
f the continental European Blue-headed
blue-grey with a white supercillium and
b-moustachial strip. The Grey-headed,
ccurring in Fenno-Scandinavia, has a dark
rey crown and nape with blackish ear-
overts. The species frequents lowland areas,
specially damp meadows, pastures with
attle and marshland edges.

 Insects, larvae and small snails.

 Constructs a nest of grass and moss
lined with hair in a grass tussock.

48 | Grey Wagtail

The Grey Wagtail has a proportionately long
tail that is constantly in motion. A rather
striking bird, it is grey above and white
below, with bright yellow on the breast and
under-tail. It is fairly common where there
are fast-flowing rivers and streams with
exposed rocks for perches. Although mainly
resident, in winter it often moves to lower
ground around lakes, slow-flowing rivers
and estuaries.

 Mainly insects and small crustaceans.

 Builds a nest of rootlets and grass
in a rock crevice, bank, bridge or
building, always situated close to
running water.

TRACK N° **47**

First the piercing, raspy buzzy *sree* song,
then liquid *tseep* calls.

TRACK N° **48**

High-pitched song and low-frequency
calls – typical for birds living near noisy rivers.
First a tinkling series of song strophes of varying
phrases of notes, then a series of rapid calls.

49 | Pied Wagtail

Pied Wagtail (left); White Wagtail (rig)

This black and white wagtail (subspecies *Motacilla alba yarrelli*) with a long, often wagged tail is a familiar sight throughout Britain, even in the hearts of cities. It is resident and found only in Britain and the near Continent. In the rest of Europe it is replaced by its close relative, the White Wagtail (subspecies *M. a. alba*), which has a pale grey rather than black back. This subspecies also occurs in Britain on passage in small numbers, particularly in spring.

On the ground the Pied Wagtail's gait is rapid, and its head is moved backwards and forwards while wagging its tail. It runs rapidly on the ground after flying insects, preferring to feed on lawns and roofs, and in car parks and roads, where its prey is easily spotted. The reasons for the near-constant tail wagging are poorly understood. It may be employed to flush prey, or to signal submissiveness to other wagtails or vigilance to potential predators.

Outside the breeding season the Pied Wagtail roosts gregariously – dozens or even hundreds of birds can often be seen going to roost in trees and on buildings in towns and cities.

Pied Wagtails are very territorial during the breeding season, when they may attack their own reflections in windows and other reflective surfaces.

 Insects.

 Constructs a nest of grass and roots, lined with animal hair, usually in a recess in a wall or building. Both sexes build the nest and incubate the eggs.

TRACK N° **49**

First the slowly advancing (with long pauses) song of *tsitsellittt* notes, then some disyllabic *tsli–vitt* calls, often given when taking flight.

0 | Dipper

British subspecies (left); northern European subspecies (right).

e Dipper is an obviously pot-bellied, short-
iled bird that inhabits fast-flowing streams
d rivers with boulders on which to perch.
ghtly Wren-like in appearance, adults are
oty-black except for a brilliant white throat
d breast. Birds in Britain and northern
ance have a rusty-brown band separating
e chest and belly. Juveniles are slate-grey.
e species is mainly resident.

Dippers occur around fast-flowing
eshwater rivers and streams, particularly
 mountains, across much of Europe. They
e usually to be seen singly or in pairs,
eferring the same stretch of water all year
und. In Britain they are fairly common in
e north and west.

Dippers are unique among songbirds in
eir ability to feed by swimming with their
ings against the current and walking on the
ream or river bottom shallows searching
r invertebrates. They can be seen bobbing
 stones in fast-flowing water, diving or

swimming, or following a stream in quick
whirring flight. Adaptations to their aquatic
habitat include relatively short and strongly
muscled wings, which may be used like
flippers underwater; dense plumage with
large preen glands for waterproofing the
feathers; sharp claws on the feet for clinging
to rocks in swift water; and nasal flaps that
stop water from getting into their nostrils.

 Insect larvae, small snails, fish eggs
and water fleas.

 Erects a large dome of moss, grass and
sedge with a side entrance, always
close to fast-flowing water and often
on masonry such as a bridge.

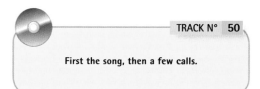

TRACK N° 50

First the song, then a few calls.

33

51 | Wren

The tiny Wren, with its stumpy cocked tail and incongruously loud song, is one of Britain's most familiar birds. It is a resident, and can suffer badly during hard winters. Found almost everywhere, from inner city gardens, forests and parks, to remote Scottish islands where it lives on cliffs, it often occurs low down in places such as thick shrubbery, brushwood piles and dry-stone walls. Normally very territorial, in winter it roosts communally with up to 20 birds crammed together in a suitable cavity.

 Small insects and spiders, with seeds in winter.

 Builds a dome of grass, leaves and lichens in a hedge, ivy, wall or shed.

52 | Dunnock

An unobtrusive sparrow-sized bird, at first sight the Dunnock appears rather drab, but closer inspection reveals that the brown-streaked upperparts, set against a lavender-grey head, breast and belly, are really quite attractive in a quiet way. Resident in Britain, it is common in both town gardens and park and rural farms with hedges and open wood feeding in leaf litter below trees and hedges It often creeps jerkily and mouse-like on the ground, quickly moving into low cover. It is also known as the Hedge Sparrow due to a slight resemblance to sparrows.

 Insects and other small invertebrates, and seeds.

 Constructs a foundation of twigs on which a cup of grass and moss is built, in a hedge or bush.

TRACK N° **51**

An amazingly loud song with trills, then rattling hard *zerrrrr* calls and sharp clicking call notes.

TRACK N° **52**

First a short song, which is often given from the top of a bush or hedge, or a wall around a garden, then the *tliihi* flight call.

53 | Common Redstart

The male Common Redstart is a slim beauty of a bird with grey upperparts and orange-red underparts especially on the breast. He has a black throat bordered white above and a flashing rusty-red tail. The female is a more dowdy brown above and rusty-buff below, but she too shares the rusty-red tail. Both sexes 'shimmer' (vibrate their tails at rest). The Common Redstart is a summer visitor from Africa, frequenting old woods, parks and large gardens in much of Europe.

 Insects and larvae, with more fruits and berries in autumn. Often feeds like a flycatcher, making aerial sallies after insects.

 Nests in holes in trees, crevices in walls and nest boxes.

54 | Robin

Probably Britain's favourite, and certainly best-known bird, the Robin is plump and upright and has a red breast that is actually more orange than red. It is familiar throughout the year in parks, gardens and woodlands. Often fearless of humans, Robins will take worms from the hand and are rarely shy, skulking only when nesting. They are resident throughout Britain, and the population is swelled in winter with arrivals from colder parts of Europe.

 Ground-dwelling insects and worms, with berries, seeds and soft fruits in autumn and winter.

 Builds a bulky nest for its size, from moss, grass and dead leaves, in a hole in a wall, shed or tree.

TRACK N° 53

First the song, then tongue-clicking *tek* calls.

TRACK N° 54

First the song, heard most of the year except in the post-breeding season. It is more eager in spring, but somewhat melancholic/wistful in autumn and winter. Then ticking call notes.

55 | Whinchat

A small and short-tailed bird, the Whinchat perches conspicuously upright on the tops of bushes and stems of vegetation. The bird's back is variegated black and brown, and the male has blackish cheeks bordered with white, and an orange-buff throat and breast. The female is similarly patterned, but less bright. A summer visitor to Britain from Africa, the Whinchat favours most types of uncultivated grassland with bushes across much of Europe. It often perches on raised spots such as telephone wires, from which it makes sallies to catch flying insects.

 Insects.

 Builds a nest of grass and moss lined with finer material in a grass tussock.

56 | Northern Wheatear

This is northern Europe's only wheatear. The male sports a handsome combination of a grey back, dark wings, white underparts, a bold black stripe through the eye bordered with white and a peachy-buff chest. The female lacks the black eye-stripe, and brownish-buff colouration replaces the grey. A summer visitor from Africa to much of Europe, the Northern Wheatear inhabits mainly treeless terrain, often perching on rocks in open country. It is familiar around British coasts on migration.

 Insects.

 Nests in a deep hole in rocks, a wall or a rabbit burrow.

TRACK N° 55

First the song, then *hii–tek tek* calls.

TRACK N° 56

First the song, then whistled *hii* and tongue–clicking *tek* calls.

Eats berries in winter (left); breast is speckled (right).

57 | Song Thrush

The Song Thrush is a familiar bird of woodland, parks and gardens, although it is more secretive than the Blackbird. It is resident, with more birds arriving in autumn from the Continent to take advantage of Britain's milder winters.

This is the brown-backed bird with a speckled breast and belly seen feeding on lawns, pulling worms from the ground. The speckles on its breast are shaped like arrowheads, and more regular than those of the Mistle Thrush. The sexes are similar, and juveniles resemble the adults. The flight is rather jerky, and its underwings show yellowish-orange.

The Song Thrush begins to sing as early as December, and has a beautiful strong song of whistling and liquid notes, rather similar to the song of a Blackbird, but it repeats each phrase, sometimes several times. A male may have a repertoire of more than a hundred phrases, copied from neighbouring birds

and its parents. The song may also include mimicry of man-made objects such as telephones.

Song Thrushes may sometimes be seen in small flocks. They are common but declining, perhaps due to the use of pesticides to control snails in gardens.

 Worms, snails and insects, with seeds and berries in winter. Uses a stone as an anvil to smash snail shells so that it can eat the contents.

 Constructs a finely woven cup of moss and grass lined with mud in a tree, bush or shed.

TRACK N° **57**

Loud song to advertise its often hidden presence in tree branches, then sharp thin *tick* calls and finally a chattering warning call near the nest.

58 | Redwing

The Redwing is a winter visitor to Britain, with large numbers sometimes arriving from Scandinavia in late September/October. It is similar to the Song Thrush, but has rusty-red flanks and under-wings, and a bright whitish stripe above the eye. The red patch is conspicuous in flight, which is fast and direct. It can be seen in flocks, often with Fieldfares and Song Thrushes, in fields or in open woods, gardens and parks where there are berry bushes. Listen for calling migrants at night.

 Worms and insects in fields, but equally fond of berries.

 The Redwing nests only occasionally in Britain.

59 | Mistle Thrush

A larger and more robust version of the Song Thrush, the Mistle Thrush is paler overall, especially on the back, which is greyish-brown. It has a markedly undulating flight like that of a woodpecker. Its habit of singing loudly from tree tops, often in poor weather, has given it the country name of Storm-cock. Mainly resident in parks, gardens and woodlands throughout Britain, it can also be found in open fields and on low moors in winter.

 Worms, snails and insects, and also ripe berries.

 Builds a cup of grass, moss and roots lined with mud and wool at varying heights in the fork of a tree.

TRACK N° 58

Two examples of the variable song, then the *chuk–chuk* (warning call) and finally the *srii* flight call.

TRACK N° 59

First the song, which is clear, loud and insistent, given from an exposed perch in a tree top, then a dry rattling call.

0 | Fieldfare

winter visitor to Britain from Scandinavia, 1e Fieldfare is of robust build, like the Mistle 1rush, but has a grey head and rump. The pots on its chest and belly are shaped like rrowheads. Its longish tail, pale grey rump nd white underwings show clearly in its 3ther flapping flight. Highly gregarious when 1 Britain, it feeds with other thrushes on 1sect-rich fields and berry-laden trees and ushes. Loud *chakk* calls when disturbed elp to identify it.

 Worms, insects, berries and fallen apples. Fond of windfall fruit.

 The Fieldfare rarely nests in Britain.

TRACK N° 60

Song not included because it is a winter visitor to Britain. Calls include a variable low cackling and *chakk* notes repeated several times in succession.

61 | Blackbird

The Blackbird is familiar throughout Britain in gardens, parks, hedgerows and woodlands. The male is unmistakable, being black all over with a bright orange-yellow bill, but his mate is a more subdued dark brown with a paler throat and breast and a blackish-brown bill. The Blackbird hops or walks over the ground, stopping and cocking its head to look for worms or other food. When disturbed it gives a loud and scolding *chink-chink*. It has a beautiful song that can be heard from February through to July.

 Worms, insects, snails, berries, soft fruits and fallen apples.

 Constructs a large cup-shaped nest of grass, moss and leaves lined with mud in a hedge, bush or small tree.

 TRACK N° 61

The stunningly beautiful fluty song, then the *srii* call, and finally the loud and hysterical *chink–chink–chink*.

62 | Reed Warbler

The Reed Warbler is a summer visitor to Britain from tropical Africa. As its name suggests, it is largely confined to reed beds during the breeding season, but on migration it can be found in a variety of damp well-vegetated situations. It is a rather nondescript brown above and buff below, and has a relatively long bill and a distinctive flat crown. It is usually seen singing as it climbs up a reed stem.

 Small aquatic insects. In autumn it feeds on berries, which provide energy for its long migratory flight.

 Constructs an intricately woven structure of grass affixed around three reed stems, which are usually growing out of water.

63 | Sedge Warbler

This small bird is brown above streaked darker, with unmarked buff-white underparts and a bold creamy stripe above the eye. It employs an oft-repeated song flight, rising vertically from vegetation with a harsh chattering, before quickly dropping back to cover again. A summer visitor to Britain from Africa, the Sedge Warbler is common where there is thick vegetation close to water, and has a preference for small ponds, ditches and marshy areas.

 Gnats, midges, aquatic insects and small molluscs. Also eats berries in autumn.

 A neat shallow cup of grass and moss is constructed in low herbage.

TRACK N° **62**
Song similar to that of Sedge Warbler, but phrases repeated in groups of three – *kek kek kek, ker ker ker, tri tri tri.*

TRACK N° **63**
The flight song, followed by the *teck* calls.

64 | Common Whitethroat

The Common Whitethroat is a small slim warbler with a longish tail. The male has a grey head, white throat and rust-coloured wings. The female lacks the grey head. The bird is a common summer visitor to Britain from Africa, abundant in areas of scrub, coastal heath and farmland with good edge cover. It can often be seen making its low and jerky song flight above a hedge or scrub, before it dives into deep cover. Although it can sometimes be very skulking, at other times it will sing quite happily from an open situation.

 Mainly insects, but also berries and fruits in autumn.

 Builds a cup of grass close to the ground in dense herbage, brambles, thick hedgerows or bushes.

65 | Lesser Whitethroat

This species has a more compact body shape and is shorter-tailed than the Common Whitethroat. It is grey-brown above and dirty-white below, and the crown is grey, with distinctly darker grey ear-coverts giving it a masked appearance. A summer visitor to Britain from north-east Africa, the Lesser Whitethroat prefers mature hedgerows in farmland, parks and even large gardens. It is secretive and can usually be located by its frequently uttered loud rattling song.

 Insects, and also fruits and berries in autumn.

 Builds a shallow and flimsy nest of grass and rootlets in a thick hedge or bush.

TRACK N° **64**

The flight song, followed by the nervous nasal *dverh-dverh-dverh* calls.

TRACK N° **65**

Song a loud far-carrying rattle on one note. Call a harsh *chek*.

66 | Garden Warbler

This very nondescript and unobtrusive warbler is greyish-brown above and paler below with no bold markings. It is quite heavily built, with a round head and short bill. It is found in woods with clearings, and parks and gardens that have large trees and good ground cover. A summer visitor to Britain from tropical Africa, it is often difficult to see due to its preference for dense cover. Garden Warblers are best detected by their song, which is loud and given from low down in dense vegetation.

 Mostly insects, and some soft fruits and berries in autumn before its migration.

 Constructs a cup of grass and hair low down in dense bushes, brambles or herbage.

67 | Blackcap

Blackcaps are mainly summer visitors to Britain from North Africa and the western Mediterranean, but increasing numbers from eastern Europe now winter here. The male is grey above with a black cap, the female brown above with a rusty-red cap. The male can be confused with the Marsh or Willow Tit, but those species have white cheeks and black chins. Blackcaps are found wherever there is broadleaved or mixed woodland, and also in large gardens in urban areas. Their loud, rich warbling song attracts the attention, but the birds are often difficult to see in the leafy canopy.

 Insects supplemented with soft fruits and berries in autumn and winter.

 Builds a tightly woven cup of grass and sedges in brambles, thick bushes or ivy.

TRACK N° 66

The song is a beautiful warble lasting a few seconds, not unlike that of the Blackcap, but almost always delivered from low dense cover. The call is an irritable *chek-chek*.

TRACK N° 67

The rich warbling song, followed by the *tack* call.

8 | Chiffchaff

69 | Willow Warbler

The Chiffchaff is a small and nondescript, dumpy warbler with greenish upperparts and off-white underparts. Its oft-repeated *chiff-chaff* song is as unremarkable as its appearance, but it is a commonly heard sound in the spring and autumn countryside, wherever the favoured habitat of open, preferably tall trees with an understorey present. Formerly only a summer visitor, increasing numbers of Chiffchaffs now winter in Britain.

This bird is like the Chiffchaff, but it is a brighter greenish-grey above and a cleaner white below, with a more noticeable whitish stripe through the eye and pale rather than dark legs. It has a beautiful song, a descending series of soft whistles, which it sings after its arrival in Britain from Africa in April. It is common where there are trees and bushes, from upland birches down to large lowland gardens.

 Aphids, small larvae and spiders picked from leaves. Chiffchaffs often sally from trees to catch flying insects.

 Almost exclusively insects, particularly aphids picked from leaves, and small caterpillars.

 Builds a domed nest of grass, dead leaves and moss in herbage, brambles or small bushes.

 Builds a dome-shaped nest of grass on or in close proximity to the ground, in good cover.

TRACK N° **68**

The repetitive *chiff–chaff, chiff–chaff* song, followed by the *hyit* call.

TRACK N° **69**

The song, followed by the *hyy–it* call, which is very similar to the call of a Chiffchaff, but slightly more up–slurred at the end.

43

70 | Wood Warbler

A little larger than the similar Willow Warbler, this is a lovely bird with moss-green upperparts, a striking lemon-yellow throat and breast, and a silky white belly. A summer visitor to Britain from Africa, seen from April to August, it prefers shaded woodland, especially that containing oak and beech, with sparse ground cover. It often stays high in the branches, but is invariably active and not secretive.

 Insects and other invertebrates, and some fruits.

 Builds a dome-shaped nest of grass lined with finer material. The nest is always well hidden in ground vegetation.

TRACK N° **70**

Both song types, the trilling song and the piping song, can be heard on the CD.

71 | Goldcrest

The Goldcrest is Britain's smallest bird. Dull green above and whitish below, a bold white wing-bar and a splendid gold (yellow in the female) crown edged with a black stripe on each side add distinction to the plumage. The bird moves constantly through the canopy, calling *zee-zee*, and outside the breeding season is often found in the company of tit flocks. It is mainly resident in Britain, and found where there are woods, parks and gardens, but has a preference for conifers, particularly yews and cypresses.

 Aphids and other small insects, found on the undersides of leaves.

 Erects a hammock of moss and lichens, which is usually hung beneath a conifer branch high in a tree.

TRACK N° **71**

Remarkably high-pitched rhythmic song, *treddle-e-dee*, repeated often and ending in a flourish. Then equally high-pitched *zee-zee, zee-zee* calls.

Adult (left); juvenile (right).

2 | Spotted Flycatcher

rather drab bird, the Spotted Flycatcher grey-brown above and dirty-white below, with – in the male – a faintly streaked crown nd breast. The female lacks the streaking. The bill and legs are black, and the black ye is an obvious feature. The tail and ings are comparatively long. Juveniles are ore speckly than the adults. The posture upright when perched.

Spotted Flycatchers usually perch nspicuously in the open on a twig or mall branch, from where they sally to catch ying insects, then often returning to the ame or a nearby perch. This characteristic, ogether with the upright pose, distinguishes em from other birds.

A summer visitor across mainland Europe om Africa, the Spotted Flycatcher is one of ritain's latest arriving migrants, rarely seen numbers until May. During the breeding eason it may be found across Britain, but is scarce in the far north and west and

virtually absent from the Scottish islands. It inhabits large gardens, orchards, parks and woodland edges.

 Insects from small flies to larger specimens such as moths, butterflies and even dragonflies.

 Builds a scruffy construction of grass and moss on the ledges of old buildings, outhouses, creepers on walls or depressions in trees. May come back to use the same nest year after year.

 TRACK N° **72**

First the simple song, then warning calls near the nest and finally 'normal' calls.

73 | Long-tailed Tit

Western European subspecies (left); northern subspecies (right

The Long-tailed Tit is an unmistakable small passerine bird that is black above and whitish below with a pinkish hue on the wings and flanks. Its body length is 13–15cm, of which 7–9cm is tail. Its shape is that of an exquisite tiny ball of fluffy feathers with an oversized tail and a minute bill.

Around 20 subspecies of Long-Tailed Tit have been recognized. The western European subspecies (*Aegithalos caudatus rosaceus*) has dark crown stripes. In northern and eastern parts of its range, the head is entirely white (subspecies *A. c. caudatus*).

The Long-tailed Tit usually travels in small, constantly calling groups. Occurring in deciduous and mixed woodland, hedgerows, parks with bushes and large gardens throughout Britain, it is mainly resident. Families form into flocks and move restlessly through woods and hedges, often with other tits, searching for insects and other small food items. In flight, which is short and consists of whirring bursts and drops, they look like tiny bouncing fluff balls with long tails. Their constant calls help to keep the flock together.

 Small insects and spiders, and seeds and fat at bird tables.

 Builds a beautifully constructed oval dome of wool, moss and lichens, woven together with spiders' webs, in the fork of a hedge or bush. Breeds deep in hedges and low cover. The young of Long-tailed Tits are raised by both parents, who may be assisted by flock members who have failed to breed.

TRACK N° 73

First a series of dry slurred *trrr* call notes and a single drawn-out, high-pitched silvery trill, then some quiet *pt* notes and finally the frequent high-pitched *ssi'ssi'ssi* note.

4 | Blue Tit

he Blue Tit is common in gardens, parks and woods throughout Britain. A tiny ball of blue and yellow with white cheeks, its acrobatics as it hangs upside down from branches and bird tables, to which it is a frequent visitor, are a source of much delight to the garden bird lover. It has small wings and a rather feeble fluttering flight. In winter it is often found in reed beds, which provide it with both food and shelter. It is mainly resident in Britain.

 Aphids and small insects supplemented with seeds, nuts, fruits and fat from bird feeders.

 Nests in a lined hole in a tree, stump, post or wall.

75 | Great Tit

This is Britain's largest tit, a mainly sedentary bird found commonly across Britain in woodland and garden habitats. It is easily identified by its yellow underparts bisected with a black band, and its black head with white cheeks. Almost as acrobatic as its smaller cousin, the Blue Tit, it is a frequent visitor to bird tables, where it is bold and aggressive. It has a bewildering variety of calls.

 Insects, small snails, worms, seeds, fruits, nuts and fat at feeders.

 Nests in a tree hole in almost any cavity, which it fills with grass, leaves and moss, and lines with hair.

TRACK N° 74

The song, including the short *tsee-tzi-tzii* and the beautiful high-pitched silvery *biibi-sisisisi-srrrrrrr*. Then various calls including *churr* notes.

TRACK N° 75

The simple song, varying a lot around the theme of *tee-ta, tee-ta, tee-ta*, then three clear syllabic *twet-twet-twe* calls, and various scolding and purring calls.

76 | Coal Tit

The Coal Tit is Britain's smallest tit, even marginally smaller than the Blue Tit. Resident throughout much of Britain, it is more closely associated with conifers than the other common tit species, and is often found with the Goldcrest. It may be seen in mixed woods, parks and large gardens with conifers. It is an attractive bird with a greyish back, buff underparts, two white wing-bars, and a black head with white cheeks and nape. Its head is relatively large, often with a slightly crested appearance.

 Insects, seeds and nuts. In the north, feeds particularly on spruce cones.

 Nests in a lined hole in a rotting tree stump.

77 | Marsh Tit

This small tit is greyish-brown above and buff-white below, with a black cap and bib and white cheeks. It is sedentary, and despite its name it does not frequent marshes, being found in damp deciduous woods, and in copses that have not been thinned and have plenty of rotten timber. It occurs across much of central and western Europe, including Britain, where it is fairly common but declining.

 Insects, seeds and berries, and visits bird feeders.

 Nests in a hole in a rotten tree trunk or stump, which it usually enlarges and lines with wool, hair and moss.

 TRACK N° **76**

Song a faster, far higher pitched version of the song of the Great Tit. Then some nasal *ty–ii* calls.

 TRACK N° **77**

Variable song – here a series of *twetwetwe...* repeated every three seconds. Diagnostic call is *shar pssi* or *pssi* chew, often with a scolding nasal *jhe jhe jhe jhe*.

8 | Treecreeper

his bird does exactly what its name
uggests, creeping mouse-like up and along,
ut never down, tree trunks and branches.
nce finished with one tree it flies down
begin a spiral up another nearby. Like no
ther British bird, it is a mixture of browns
nd buffs above and whitish below, and has
very small body with a comparatively long
nd thin down-curved bill, and a long spiked
il that it presses against a tree for support.
is resident in Britain and found almost
verywhere in wooded country. In winter
often roams with tit flocks.

 Almost exclusively small insects,
but also occasionally seeds.

 Nest is built on a supporting platform
of small twigs behind the loose bark
of a tree or in ivy.

TRACK N° 78
A quiet but distinctive *swee-swee-swee*
song followed by a trill, then the *tsree* call
and finally a very thin, high-pitched *tih* call.

79 | Nuthatch

An attractive bird, the Nuthatch is steel
blue-grey above and rusty-buff below,
and has a distinctive black eye-stripe and
a relatively long and sharply pointed bill.
Scandinavian birds are white below. The
Nuthatch announces its presence in the tree
canopy with loud ringing calls. It is resident
and common in much of England and Wales
in deciduous or mixed woods, open parkland
and large gardens near woodland, but largely
absent from Scotland and Ireland. It has the
unique ability among Britain's birds to run up
or down tree trunks and large branches.

 Mainly spiders and insects, including
beetles and grubs in summer. Nuts and
larger seeds in autumn and winter.

 Nests in a hole in a tree trunk or wall
with leaves, grass and bark. If the hole
is too large it is blocked with mud until
the required size is achieved.

TRACK N° 79
Two different song types, a rapid
liquid trilling, *ve've've've've'*, then a slow
disyllabic *wee-wee* repeated every few seconds
or so. Calls include an often-repeated *tuiep*.

80 | Starling

Non-breeding plumage (left); breeding plumage (right)

The Starling is resident throughout Britain, but in winter there is a big immigration from colder climes to the north and east. It is then that the spectacle of huge flocks of birds can be observed in aerial display before they go to roost in trees and reed beds, and on city buildings. In some parts of Europe, roosts can comprise up to 1.5 million birds. In Britain, flocks (commonly called 'moots') can number 50,000 birds, and form just before sunset in mid-winter. Starlings are extremely sociable in all seasons.

In non-breeding birds, the iridescent black feathers have clear pale spots, which are reduced in breeding birds. The bill is yellow in breeding birds, otherwise blackish, in the male with a blue base, and the legs are pinkish. The throat feathers are long and loose, and used in displays. Juveniles are unspotted and variably light to dark grey-brown. The flight profile of Starlings is triangular.

Starlings walk and do not hop, and have a relatively strong and direct flight. Like many species in their family, they are good mimics.

 Insects, particularly crane-fly larvae, spiders and worms supplemented by seeds, soft fruits and cereals. Feeds mostly on the ground, prying with its bill to search for hidden food items.

 Nests in holes, usually in walls or buildings, but also in trees and cliffs.

TRACK N° 80

First the song, a rich rambling collection of rather strangled sounds, throaty warblings and musical whistles, including much mimicry. Then *thceerr* calls from a flock.

81 | Jay

This is one of the most striking of British birds, quite unlike other members of the crow family. It is pinkish-brown with blue and white in the wings, a white rump and throat, a black moustache, and a streaked black and white erectile crown. Jays are resident in Britain, but common only where there is good woodland cover, even in parks and large gardens. They are partial to acorns, which they hoard for winter in the autumn, and favour oak woods.

 Omnivorous, feeding on seeds, fruits, birds' eggs, nestlings and insects.

 Builds a well-hidden untidy platform of twigs and roots in the fork of a tree or bush.

82 | Magpie

An unmistakable large black and white crow with a very long tail, the Magpie is a common resident in a wide variety of habitats, including urban areas. Its wings are a metallic blue-black, and its tail has a green sheen. The male is larger than the female, and often tends to have a longer tail. The Magpie often lives near humans, having learned to recognize them as a source of easy food pickings and protection from predators.

 Eats virtually anything – carrion, scraps, nestlings, worms, insects, fruits and seeds.

 Constructs a huge domed nest of sticks that is very visible in a tree or large bush when leaf cover is absent.

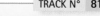

TRACK N° **81**

A variety of calls – here first strange conversational clucking notes, then a *chewchewchewchew...* series, and finally some common harsh and raucous calls.

TRACK N° **82**

Magpies have a range of calls. The CD includes first a staccato chattering, then sharp *ch'chack* calls.

83 | Jackdaw

This small and compact black crow can be recognized by its grey nape and pale eye. It struts as it walks, and in flight its wingbeats are faster and deeper than those of the Carrion Crow. It is very gregarious and can often be seen in wheeling flocks, especially in the evenings before it goes to roost communally. It is resident in Britain and common everywhere – farmland, parks, towns, ruins and coastal cliffs.

 Insects and worms, but also eggs and nestlings, and fruits and corn in autumn.

 Nests colonially in cracks and holes in woods, on cliff faces, and in ruins and chimneys.

84 | Rook

The adults of this glossy black crow can easil be distinguished from the similar Carrion Crow by the extensive area of greyish-white bare skin above the bill, and by the loose feathering around the thighs that give them a baggy-trousered look. The Rook is resident in Britain and has a close association with humans, nesting colonially in isolated patche of trees, often in churchyards, on farmland, and around villages and rural towns. It feeds on the ground in pasture and arable land, employing a waddling gait like that of a duck

 Insects, worms and some vegetable matter, especially corn.

 Nests in a rookery, building a large and very obvious stick nest.

TRACK N° 83

Typical *tjakk*, *khakk* or *kyak* calls, first from a group of birds near a breeding colony, then from a single individual.

TRACK N° 84

Harsh and hoarse *graah* calls by a couple of individuals, then a near–deafening cacophany of sound from a rookery.

Carrion Crow (left); Hooded Crow (right).

85 | Carrion Crow

The Carrion Crow is about the size of a Rook, but black all over with a purple sheen, a stout bill, and no particular distinguishing marks, and generally more solitary in behaviour. It does not breed in colonies and is common in town parks, unlike the Rook. The two species may, however, feed together, and Carrion Crows are often sociable in winter roosts.

Resident in Britain and catholic in choice of habitat, the Carrion Crow is found in towns and woods, and on farmland, moors and sea cliffs. It is replaced in eastern and northern Europe, including the north of Scotland and Ireland, by the closely related Hooded Crow, a more striking black and grey bird. It has a black head with a black bill and eyes, and a black throat, wings, tail and thigh feathers, and feet. The remainder of the plumage is ash-grey in colour.

When first hatched, the young are much blacker than their parents. The plumage of juveniles is duller, and they have bluish or greyish eyes. Where the Carrion Crow and Hooded Crow overlap, they may breed.

 Omnivorous, feeding on carrion, nestlings and eggs, grain and insects. May harass birds of prey and even foxes for their kills, and cooperate with other crows to make kills. Scavengers by nature, crows often frequent sites inhabited by humans in order to feed on their household waste. Both species may drop molluscs and other shelled animals from a height in order to break them open.

 Constructs a bulky scruffy platform of sticks high up in a tall tree or large bush or cliff ledge. Offspring from previous years may stay around and help rear new hatchlings. The eggs are incubated by the female, who is fed by the male.

TRACK N° 85

Very vocal, commonly heard call being *kraah* with some variation.

86 | House Sparrow

As its name suggests, the House Sparrow is a bird of built-up areas that has become very much tied to humans, to the extent that we have become the limiting factor in its distribution. It is brown streaked darker above and greyish-white below, and often looks rather scruffy, but the male does have a smart black bib and a grey crown. House Sparrows are resident everywhere humans have built their homes and factories, although they have recently declined in some parts of Britain.

 Seeds, insects and household scraps, especially bread.

 Nests under roof tiles, in gutters, on ledges on buildings or, more rarely, in trees and bushes.

87 | Tree Sparrow

This bird is similar to but more handsome than the House Sparrow. It has generally brighter hues with a red-brown rather than grey crown, a black spot on the white cheek patch and a white band across the nape. The sexes are alike. A resident of open farmland, in summer it breeds on the edges of small woods; in winter it frequents farm fields, where it feeds on seeds and spilt grain, often in the company of finches and buntings.

 Seeds, but will also take insects. May visit bird tables.

 Constructs an untidy structure of grass in a hole in a tree or building, usually colonially. Readily adopts nest boxes.

TRACK N° **86**

The song is frequently interpreted as *chirp–chirp*, but is in fact *tselp–tselp*.

TRACK N° **87**

First the simple song of repeated *chelp* notes, then a mixture of mono and disyllabic calls, and finally a mixture of *chilp* and rattling notes.

Male (left); female (right).

38 | Bullfinch

This is a large plump finch with a stubby bill, usually seen in pairs or small parties that are rarely into double figures.

The male Bullfinch has a bluish-grey back, reddish-pink underparts, a black cap, a black tail and a white rump, and is undoubtedly one of Britain's most attractive birds. The female is similarly patterned to the male, but in more subdued hues, with a pale brown breast. Juveniles have a grey-brown head and breast. White wingbars of both sexes show in flight, which is fast and undulating. Northern European birds are larger and brighter than those occurring in southern Europe.

A retiring bird, the Bullfinch is most frequently seen as a white rump fast disappearing into a hedgerow or bush.

Bullfinches are found everywhere with the exception of the far north, in scrub, rural gardens with Blackthorn or fruit trees, churchyards, orchards and forest edges. They are widespread and resident in most parts of Europe except the far south, although they are declining, possibly due to a decrease in woodland areas.

 Seeds in autumn and winter, the buds of trees in spring, and insects and larvae in the breeding season.

 Constructs an intricate platform of woven sticks, roots and moss, which is usually well hidden in a hedgerow, bush or brambles.

TRACK N° 88

The male's song, which is not often heard, is a rambling twittering without clear phrases. The call is a piping single note given singly or in a series of 2–3 notes.

89 | Chaffinch

Male (left); female (right)

Mainly resident, the Chaffinch is Britain's most common finch and one of Britain's most common birds, found everywhere where there are open woods, hedges, parks and gardens. In winter its numbers swell with visitors from the north, and it frequents farmland with other finches and sparrows.

The male Chaffinch is a handsome colourful bird sporting rusty-red cheeks and breast, and a blue-grey crown and neck. In winter the blue-grey and rusty-red colours are subdued. Its bill is grey-blue in summer, turning to pale brown in winter. The female (and also juveniles) is a rather drab brown, somewhat similar to a female House Sparrow, but she has a prominent double white bar on the wing and a greenish rump that can be seen when she takes flight.

The Chaffinch's song is powerful, and male birds typically sing two or three different song types.

Although Chaffinches are found in many types of habitat, they do appear to be decreasing in Britain, perhaps due to weed control on farmland that reduces their food supply.

 Seeds and grain, with insects including caterpillars during the breeding season. Chaffinches have the widest diet of all the finches.

 Builds a superbly woven cup of moss and lichens, bound with spiders' webs, usually in the fork of a tree, hedge or bush. The female incubates the eggs and the young are fed by both parents.

TRACK N° **89**

The cheerful song, then a *twink* (*pink, fink*) call and an upwards-inflected clear *hwet.*

90 | Greenfinch

This sturdy green finch has a heavy bill, a yellow wing-panel and yellow sides to the tail that are conspicuous in flight. The female and juvenile are paler with streaking, which is stronger in juveniles. The flight is bounding and undulating. The Greenfinch is resident everywhere in Britain in relatively open habitat with some trees and bushes. The birds often perch on the tops of trees and bushes, attracting attention with their persistent nasal calls.

 Seeds and berries, but feeds its young on insects.

 Constructs a loose structure of twigs and grass lined with moss in a bush, tree or overgrown hedge.

91 | Goldfinch

The Goldfinch is a most attractive bird that was once much prized by the cage-bird trade. The sexes are alike, with stunning red, black and white heads and ivory-coloured bills. The juvenile has a brown-streaked head. In flight the wings show broad golden bands, and the white rump and black tail are visible. Mainly resident in Britain, Goldfinches are found everywhere where there are parks, large gardens, orchards and areas of scrub close to woodland edges.

 A specialized bill enables the Goldfinch to extract seeds from thistles and teasels, its main food source.

 Builds a neat cup of roots filled with moss, lichens and thistledown in a tree, large bush or dense hedge.

TRACK N° **90**

Two song types – a nasal downwards–inflected *djeeeeuuoo* (*sruuuoooo*), then a more complex song with slower notes – *djuw, djuw djuw, jup jup jup, chi'di'di'di'di.*

TRACK N° **91**

A vocal bird with a variety of calls, here a bright, fast, tinkling rattling and trilling song, which is quite complex and usually recognizable by the inclusion of call notes.

92 | Siskin

Male (left); female (right)

A small green and yellow finch with streaking, the male Siskin has a smart black crown and bib, and is more yellow in colour than the female. The wingbars in both sexes are yellow, and the male's tail has patches on either side.

The Siskin's flight is flitting and uneven, and outside the breeding season the birds stay together in close flocks. They appear tit-like and very agile on the outer twigs of alders and birches when foraging, and may be found with redpolls, which also favour these trees.

Siskins breed in areas with pine or spruce. At other times they are found in a wider variety of habitats, but particularly in areas with birch and alder, on which they feed. They are not common residents, but many from northern and eastern Europe spend the winter in Britain. Until the 19th century, Siskins bred in only a few places in Scotland. Their British range has expanded considerably due to the planting of commercial conifer plantations, although they are still uncommon in the south and east of England.

 The sharply pointed bill is ideal for extracting the seeds of various trees – particularly those of alder and conifers – which provide the bulk of the Siskin's diet. Food in the breeding season includes insects.

 Constructs a nest from fir twigs lined with moss and hair, usually at a considerable height in a pine or spruce tree.

TRACK N° 92

First the song, a rapid undulating trilling, twittering and repeated call notes, plus a strangled, drawn-out nasal wheeze. Then some downwards-inflected clear *dju'ii* calls.

93 | Lesser Redpoll

The Lesser Redpoll is a small and rather nondescript grey and brown finch, but capped with a splendid red fore-crown, or 'poll', and with a small black bib and a tiny yellow bill. In spring the male also sports a pinkish-red throat and breast. The wings have faint wingbars. Juveniles lack the red head, and have less black on the chin than the adults.

Lesser Redpolls are mainly resident in Britain, with numbers being augmented from the north in winter. The birds are sociable, and flocks form in winter, especially in alders and birches. They feed mainly on trees, but also on the ground, especially in winter when the seed supply becomes reduced.

Lesser Redpolls are generally distributed where there are extensive areas of birch, alder, willow and young conifers, but are nowhere common and have declined in recent decades.

The Mealy Redpoll, a rare winter visitor from northern Europe to the north and east of Britain, is very similar to the Lesser Redpoll, but its plumage is paler and less brown in colour.

 Seeds, especially those of birch, alder and grasses, and also fruit buds and invertebrates.

 Builds a small cup of grass and moss high in a tree or bush. Nest is built by the female, and she incubates the eggs while being fed by the male.

TRACK N° 93

First a series of long, rolling buzzing notes, *dzhiiirrrrr*, then slowly repeated *chechechecheche* calls.

59

94 | Linnet

Male in breeding plumage (left); female (right)

For much of the year the male Linnet is a plain brown and grey bird, but in spring he develops an attractive grey head and a crimson-red fore-crown and breast. The female and juveniles have streaked upperparts and flanks, and a duller colouration.

Linnets are found almost everywhere where there is open ground with thick bushes, especially gorse and thorn. In winter they can also be found in fields, on rough and derelict ground, and in coastal marshes. They are resident in most parts of Britain, and widespread throughout much of Europe.

Linnets are sociable outside the breeding season, occurring in restless, constantly moving flocks, which may be mixed with other finches.

Although the Linnet is still a common species, it is declining because of changes in agricultural practices such as the use of herbicides, scrub removal and excessive hedge trimming. It was once popular as a cage bird, being valued as such because of its beautiful sweet song, which is rather like that of a canary, consisting of chirping and rolling sounds.

 Seeds of various plants, often weeds, although Linnets depend less on this food source that do most other British finches.

 Builds a nest of fine twigs, grass and wool in a bush, especially gorse, or thick ground cover.

TRACK N° 94

First the varied song of male, a series of call-type notes interspersed with more musical whistles. Then the nasal staccato *chd'it chd'it* call.

95 | Yellowhammer

In summer the male Yellowhammer has a bright yellow head and breast; in winter the yellow is less evident, as in the female at all times. Otherwise the plumage is heavily streaked and chestnut-brown. Yellowhammers are mainly resident in Britain and widely distributed in open bushy country, but have decreased alarmingly in recent decades, partly due to the reduction in hedgerows. They form small flocks in winter and forage around farmyards and stubble, often with sparrows and finches.

 Seeds, grain and fruits, with insects in summer.

 Builds a nest of grass and moss on or near the ground, on vegetated banks, in brambles or in hedgerow bottoms.

TRACK N° 95

Song, often quoted as a fast 'a little bit of bread' followed by a slow 'and no cheese'. Then the call, *djih*.

96 | Reed Bunting

The breeding male Reed Bunting is unmistakable, with a black head and throat, and a white moustache and neck collar, but in winter only vestiges of this distinctive plumage remain and he becomes a basically brown-above, white-below bird, streaked darker all over, like the female. Reed Buntings are resident in Britain and widely distributed wherever there are reed stands, marshes and bushy areas with damp ground. In winter they are often found – along with other buntings and sparrows – around farmland, where food is easier to find.

 Mainly insects in summer, and seeds and grain in winter.

 Forms a nest of grass, reed blades and moss close to the ground in a tussock or low bush.

TRACK N° 96

Rapid song by unpaired male, then a slower halting, barely musical version with pauses between notes. Calls include a downwards-inflected *tseeou* and a nasal rasping *djuh*.

61

SPECIES LIST

	PAGE No	TRACK No		PAGE No	TRACK No
Blackbird *Turdus merula*	39	61	Coot *Fulica atra*	17	20
Blackcap *Sylvia atricapilla*	42	67	Cuckoo *Cuculus canorus*	25	36
Black-headed Gull *Chroicocephalus ridibundus*	22	30	Curlew *Numenius arquata*	20	25
Blue Tit *Cyanistes caeruleus*	47	74	Dipper *Cinclus cinclus*	33	50
Bullfinch *Pyrrhula pyrrhula*	55	88	Dunlin *Calidris alpina*	19	24
Carrion Crow, Hooded Crow *Corvus corone, C. cornix*	53	85	Dunnock *Prunella modularis*	34	52
Chaffinch *Fringilla coelebs*	56	89	Feral Pigeon *Columba livia* var. *domestica*	24	33
Chiffchaff *Phylloscopus collybita*	43	68	Fieldfare *Turdus pilaris*	39	60
Coal Tit *Periparus ater*	48	76	Gadwall *Anas strepera*	10	7
Collared Dove *Streptopelia decaocto*	25	35	Garden Warbler *Sylvia borin*	42	66
Common Buzzard *Buteo buteo*	14	13	Goldcrest *Regulus regulus*	44	71
Common Redstart *Phoenicurus phoenicurus*	35	53	Golden Plover *Pluvialis apricaria*	18	22
Common Sandpiper *Actitis hypoleucos*	21	27	Goldfinch *Carduelis carduelis*	57	91
Common Swift *Apus apus*	26	38	Great Crested Grebe *Podiceps cristatus*	6	1
Common Tern *Sterna hirundo*	23	31	Great Spotted Woodpecker *Dendrocopos major*	27	40
Common Whitethroat *Sylvia communis*	41	64	Great Tit *Parus major*	47	75

SPECIES LIST

 PAGE No | TRACK No   PAGE No | TRACK No

Species	PAGE No	TRACK No
Greenfinch *Carduelis chloris*	57	90
Green Woodpecker *Picus viridis*	27	39
Grey Heron *Ardea cinerea*	7	3
Grey Partridge *Perdix perdix*	16	17
Grey Wagtail *Motacilla cinerea*	31	48
Hobby *Falco subbuteo*	14	14
House Martin *Delichon urbicum*	29	43
House Sparrow *Passer domesticus*	34	86
Jackdaw *Corvus monedula*	52	83
Jay *Garrulus glandarius*	51	81
Kestrel *Falco tinnunculus*	15	15
Lapwing *Vanellus vanellus*	19	23
Lesser Redpoll, Mealy Redpoll *Carduelis cabaret, C. flammea*	59	93
Lesser Whitethroat *Sylvia curruca*	41	65
Linnet *Carduelis cannabina*	60	94
Little Grebe *Tachybaptus ruficollis*	6	2

Species	PAGE No	TRACK No
Little Ringed Plover *Charadrius dubius*	18	21
Long-tailed Tit *Aegithalos caudatus*	46	73
Magpie *Pica pica*	51	82
Mallard *Anas platyrhynchos*	9	5
Marsh Tit *Poecile palustris*	48	77
Meadow Pipit *Anthus pratensis*	30	46
Mistle Thrush *Turdus viscivorus*	38	59
Moorhen *Gallinula chloropus*	17	19
Mute Swan *Cygnus olor*	8	4
Northern Wheatear *Oenanthe oenanthe*	36	56
Nuthatch *Sitta europaea*	49	79
Pheasant *Phasianus colchicus*	15	16
Pied Wagtail *Motacilla alba*	32	49
Pochard *Aythya ferina*	12	10
Redshank *Tringa totanus*	20	26
Redwing *Turdus iliacus*	38	58

SPECIES LIST

 PAGE No TRACK No

 PAGE No TRACK No

Species	PAGE No	TRACK No
Reed Bunting *Emberiza schoeniclus*	61	96
Reed Warbler *Acrocephalus scirpaceus*	40	62
Robin *Erithacus rubecula*	35	54
Rook *Corvus frugilegus*	52	84
Sand Martin *Riparia riparia*	29	44
Sedge Warbler *Acrocephalus schoenobaenus*	40	63
Shoveler *Anas clypeata*	10	8
Siskin *Carduelis spinus*	58	92
Skylark *Alauda arvensis*	28	41
Snipe *Gallinago gallinago*	22	29
Song Thrush *Turdus philomelos*	37	57
Sparrowhawk *Accipiter nisus*	13	12
Spotted Flycatcher *Muscicapa striata*	45	72
Starling *Sturnus vulgaris*	30	80
Stock Dove *Columba oenas*	23	32
Swallow *Hirundo rustica*	28	42

Species	PAGE No	TRACK No
Tawny Owl *Strix aluco*	26	37
Teal *Anas crecca*	11	9
Treecreeper *Certhia familiaris*	49	78
Tree Pipit *Anthus trivialis*	30	45
Tree Sparrow *Passer montanus*	54	87
Tufted Duck *Aythya fuligula*	12	11
Water Rail *Rallus aquaticus*	16	18
Whinchat *Saxicola rubetra*	36	55
Wigeon *Anas penelope*	9	6
Willow Warbler *Phylloscopus trochilus*	43	69
Woodcock *Scalopax rusticola*	21	28
Woodpigeon *Columba palumbus*	24	34
Wood Warbler *Phylloscopus sibilatrix*	44	70
Wren *Troglodytes troglodytes*	34	51
Yellowhammer *Emberiza citrinella*	61	95
Yellow Wagtail *Motacilla flava*	31	47